LET'S MURDER VIVALDI

A Play

by

DAVID MERCER

LONDON
SAMUEL FRENCH LIMITED

Printed in Great Britain by
Biddles Ltd, Guildford, Surrey.

CAST

Ben
Julie
Monica
Gerald
A Hotel Waiter

SCENE 1

A shabby flat in Camden Town — one very large room with a kitchen off. A few simple, second-hand pieces of furniture. A long, solid table with drawing board and instruments — a draughtsman's tools. A lot of books in stacks and rows. A woman's clothes and shoes are scattered in various places. In one corner, a small upright piano with music open on it. Near it, a music stand, a chair and a stool with a violin and bow on it. It is evening. The room is in shadow, lit only by an angle-poise lamp on the table with its shade close to the wall. Ben, a man in his late twenties, sits hunched by the gas fire drinking whisky. His back is to the door. He gets up once, lifts the violin and bow from the stool, half begins to play. He puts it down and resumes his former position. The door opens and Julie enters, a girl of twenty-five. She hesitates in the doorway looking at Ben. He doesn't turn round. She gropes for the light switch

Ben	Don't turn that bloody light on!
	She closes the door and comes uncertainly into the living room
Julie	Ben —
Ben	Get out. Get back wherever you've been. *(Turning)* With whoever you've been.
	Pause
Julie	I haven't. You know I haven't.
Ben	Do I?
	Julie crosses to a smaller table where Ben has recently had a meal. Stares at it
Julie	I'm hungry.
	With a sudden quick movement Ben goes to the cupboard where Julie keeps her clothes. He piles some of them into the middle of the floor. She watches, impassive

Ben   Come on. Get your stuff and get out.
                 He takes a suitcase off the cupboard top and
                 throws it among the clothes

Julie   I didn't finish work till seven.
                 He goes to a record rack, starts pulling out the
                 records and throwing them onto the floor

Ben   Which are yours? I don't know. Take the lot. *(He seems*
            to suddenly weary of his own mood and speaks gently)
            I'm tone deaf. I like a good brass band. *(Pause)* Don't I?
                 Julie turns away, crosses to a chair, sits down

Julie   A man was pushing against me in the tube. *(Pause)* I
            stood on his foot. He just stared at me and went on
            writhing about. *(Pause)* Why can't I ever say anything to
            them? Something loud and rude. *(Pause)* I never can.
                 Pause

Ben   Poor sod.
                 Pause

Julie   Him or me?
                 Ben goes to his work table and picks up a pair
                 of shear-like scissors

Ben   Him.
                 Pause

Julie   He had bad breath as well.

Ben   What you need for the tube love is a pair of scissors. A
            pair of big sharp scissors.
                 He snaps the scissors and throws them back on
                 the table

Ben   Chop their cobblers off. Serve them right. Those nasty
            men. Aren't they nasty men? Fancying you like that?
            (Pause) It's notorious, is the Northern Line. *(Pause)*
            Bakerloo's a runner-up. *(Pause)* Where've you really
            been?

Julie   They do it to ugly girls as well.

Ben   Where've you been?

Julie   If you really want me to leave —

Ben   *(raging)* Naturally I want you to leave! I'm tired of you.
            Bored with you. *(Pause)* I never *see* you, do I?

Julie   I'd bought a joint. I was going to make you a nice supper.

Ben   What — to *placate* me?

Julie   I swore if you threw my clothes out once more — I'd go.

Ben   Well then.

Julie   You're always so *angry*. *Is* it me? Do I make you like that?

Ben   I've been bad tempered ever since I was old enough to throw a rattle.

Julie   Well look. I mean, just look. What you've done with my things.

> *Decisively, she gets up, takes a carrier which she had brought in with her and goes into the kitchen*

Julie   *I'm* not going to hang them up again.

> *She unpacks the carrier, putting various things away. Unwraps the joint, puts it on a plate. Ben comes to the doorway*

Ben   If you'd only admit you don't want to go on. Just *admit* it.

Julie   Are people bad tempered for no reason? All their lives? *(She goes up to him quizzically)* Were you breast fed?

Ben   How the hell do I know?

Julie   Ask your mother. Ask her.

> *She tumbles some potatoes into the bowl and starts peeling*

Julie   And pick my things up.

Ben   You aren't bad tempered are you? Certainly not. I *will* admit. *(Pause)* You're bloody *passive*. No wonder you went into the Civil Service —

Julie   I don't see the connection —

Ben   Where does he live? What's he like? What *are* senior civil servants like? *(Pause)* He's married. He's got children. He lives in Potter's Bar.

> *Julie turns to him stonily*

Julie   He lives in St. John's Wood — and I'm *not* having an affair with him.

Ben   Potter's Bar.

Julie   St. John's *Wood!*

Ben   You've been there. Met his wife. Patted his kids. She's fair-haired. In a bun. Going a bit grey. A bit heavy. Fleshy. She's very quiet and she just sits there placidly

after the pair of you've washed up. Whilst *he* plays that
bloody Bartok record he got in Budapest when he was
sniffing round their town planning department. *(Pause)*
I'm on to the lot of you.

Julie   Ben —

Ben   What?

Julie   *Stop* it. Please.
                    Pause

Ben   I hate you.
                    *He goes back into the sitting room. Julie goes
                    on peeling potatoes*

Ben   I'll bet she's called Alice. And she knows he knocks off
          girls at the office. But she's *sensible* about it. *(Picks up a
          newspaper)* They have more enduring things in common
          than sex. What about gardening? I'll bet they spend
          Sundays burrowing about like a couple of bloody moles.
          (Pause) They'll be experts. Know all the different
          flowers . . . contact with nature in the midst of urban
          squalor . . . to say nothing of well-organised dinner
          parties.
                    *With a crunch, a potato rips the newspaper
                    from his fingers. Julie stands in the kitchen
                    doorway looking pleased with herself. Ben
                    picks the potato from his lap and holds it up*

Ben   You've slept with him.

Julie   I haven't.

Ben   You've been out with him.

Julie   Once or twice for a drink. That's all.

Ben   And in the office? In the evenings? When the rats have
          abandoned the sinking ship of state for the night?

Julie   In the *office*?

Ben   On the floor. They get carpets at his rank don't they?
          (Pause) On the floor. *(Pause)* I'll bet he's had a few of
          you down on that floor. *(Pause)* Murmuring bits of
          Rimbaud as the twilight falls over Horse Guards Parade —

Julie   He hasn't even *touched* me.
                    Pause

Ben   Shall we start a kid tonight?
                    Pause

Julie	I've told you. You're completely unrealistic about it.
Ben	*Why* am I?
Julie	Because look at us. Listen to us.

Ben dives for the pile of clothing, grabs two or three dresses and makes for the window. As he reaches it and heaves at the sash

| Ben | This bloody lot's going out — |
| Julie | If you do that — *I* shall go. |

Very deliberately, Ben lifts the sash and hurls out the dresses. Pulls the window down. Turns to her

| Ben | Blow, then — |

He picks up the suitcase and throws it at her. It crashes at her feet. She stands looking at it

Julie	I haven't slept with him. You know you trust me. Why do you *(pointing at the mess on the floor)* need all this?
Ben	*Need* it? *Me*? *Need* it? You're the one that needs it. The only form of communication you can understand is emotional extravagance. It's *you* needs it love! I suppose you *were* breast fed? Well. If you're a living example of what breasts can *do* for somebody —
Julie	If I slept with another man, you'd be relieved — wouldn't you? You're *desperate* for it. Why does my not wanting somebody else *frustrate* you so much?
Ben	You know what? You live in a fog of self-deception.
	Pause
Julie	I wouldn't mind being married.
Ben	Not *that* again. Please. I mean — you're the one that thinks being married or not married is an irrelevance!
Julie	Yes. That's what I think.
Ben	Yes. Well, it's bloody well what *I* think.
Julie	I just thought maybe we ought to get married.
Ben	I suppose it's one way of expressing a sense of total failure.

Julie kneels and begins to bundle her remaining dresses into her case

| Julie | I see. That's it then. So I'll go. *(Pause)* You'd better turn the oven off. |
| Ben | Go where? |

Julie	Anywhere.
Ben	*Where?*
Julie	Off you go again! Irritation posing as concern. That's you.

> *Ben sits down and watches her fumbling with the clothes*

Ben	I might *not* turn the oven off. I might put me head in it.
Julie	With the jets lit?
Ben	There's nothing makes me feel more vicious than watching you pack.
Julie	It's quite simple. The only times I pack — I'm grovelling about on the floor with stuff you've chucked down. It makes you feel guilty. *(She kneels back a moment, looking at him)* I know every phase you go through on these occasions. Only one thing. This time I *am* going, and this time we can do without the knife bit.

> *She is folding a skirt with her head bent low, Ben leaps for her, grabs a handful of her hair . . . wraps it round his hand . . . raises her head with it*

Ben	Can we?
	Pause
Julie	If you *believe* I'm going — you won't start on that.

> *He lets go of her hair, rushes into the kitchen — comes back with a thin sharp butcher's knife*

Julie	I'm not frightened, Ben. This time you look — silly.
Ben	You're not going —
	Pause
Julie	I'm really tired of it. That's all I can say.
Ben	I wish you were ugly —
Julie	If I was . . . and you loved me . . . it'd still be the same. *(Pause)* I know you love me. *(Pause)* But you choke the life out of me. *(Pause)* Living with you . . . I just seem to be a kind of endless provocation to you. I don't know how . . . or why. I just know that's what I am. *(Pause)* I don't think anybody's ever made me feel so helpless.

> *Ben fingers the knife blade. He is almost trembling*

Ben	You think I wouldn't mark you?

	She closes the case and stands up facing him
Julie	Go on, then —
Ben	I look silly, do I?
	Pause
Julie	No.
Ben	You'll say anything to calm me down, won't you?
Julie	I doubt if I *can* calm you —
Ben	Do you lie to me?
Julie	Never over anything important.
Ben	It depends what you mean important, doesn't it?
	Pause
Julie	I mean, I wouldn't ever lie about something where you needed the truth.
Ben	You sanctimonious twat!
	Pause
Julie	I suppose so.
Ben	You're not going.
Julie	I think — I am.
Ben	You don't give me a single thing I want.
	Pause
Julie	No.
Ben	What do we live together *for*?
Julie	If you want to buy a house. And put a woman in it. And get her pregnant. *(Pause)* Get on with it.
	Ben is rigid, holding the knife. Julie backs away. She finds her coat, picks up the case. He is completely immobile. She goes to the door
Ben	Julie —
Julie	I'm off, Ben.
Ben	Julie —
	Pause
Julie	You can't believe it, can you? It isn't me, is it? I never *do* go do I? *(Pause)* I don't bloody well exist — do I?
	She reaches for the doorknob and opens the door. As she does so, Ben hurtles across the room and pulls her back by one arm. She turns to him. He rakes the knife down one side of

*her face. The shock even prevents her screaming.
She touches her face. Her hand comes away
wet with blood. She rushes out leaving her
case, the door open—Ben looking at the knife.
He goes onto the landing—looks downstairs.
We hear a door slam. He goes back in. The door
closes quietly behind him*

SCENE 2

*A comfortable, smart flat in St. John's Wood.
Off the large main room, a dining section at
right angles. Gerald, a thin rather tired looking
man in his mid-forties, and his wife Monica,
are having coffee after dinner. She is pouring
herself a brandy. She is about his age—dark,
vivid, a bony attractive face and a forceful,
intelligent presence. She pushes the brandy
bottle across to him and lights a cigarette*

Monica	What's *he* like?
Gerald	I've never met him. He sounds rather hysterical.
Monica	*She* makes him sound hysterical.
Gerald	I mean—that's the impression I have.
	Pause
Monica	Shall we not talk about it?
Gerald	It's a form of self-indulgence you don't *usually* spare yourself.
Monica	What does he do?
Gerald	I believe he's a draughtsman.
Monica	You "believe"!
Gerald	He's a draughtsman.
Monica	Whenever you start saying "I believe" or "I imagine" or "there's some possibility" or "it could be likely"—it always means that you *know*. Definitely.
Gerald	He's twenty-eight. Born in Hull, like Julie. Wanted to be a violinist. Didn't. And I assure you she *is* evasive on that subject. *(Pause)* Father a drayman for a brewery . . . now let me think. Is there anything else? *(Pause)* Yes. *(Pause)* She says he's violent.

Monica   Which means *she's* a masochist.

Gerald   Does it?

Monica   I imagine there's some possibility.

Pause

Gerald   If you think I'm having an affair with Julie—

Monica   What's his name?

Gerald   Ben.

Monica   Ben.

Gerald   Yes. Do you like that as a name?

Monica   I can't say I like Julie.

Gerald   But you like *her*—

Monica   Oh yes. I like *her.* The ones you bring here are always nice. *(Pause)* She's perhaps a shade . . . dissociated.

Gerald   Eh?

Monica   Isn't that a good word?

Gerald   I do know it.

Monica   Yes. I know it too. Incoherent girls always like you best. I mean—fragmented ones. A bit for you. A bit for me. A bit for them. *(Pause)* A bit for Ben?

Gerald   I see. Dissociated.

Monica   Women who are all of a piece know that you know they're the most troublesome. It makes them realistic. Besides, I think your *particular* kind of charm thrives on muddleheadedness.

Gerald   Why does it do that?

Monica   I don't want you to think I underestimate Julie.

Gerald   I don't really mind. If I *were* having an affair with her I might get tetchy on that score.

Monica   I can see that you have to love them to make it work. You must have loved an extraordinary number of girls by now.

Gerald   To make what work?

Monica   To justify the consequences to yourself of having an affair. *(Pause)* And the imagined consequences for me. *(Pause)* But I think I've always been rather cheerful, haven't I?

Gerald   Indefatigably.

Pause

Monica	Makes you suspicious.
Gerald	Naturally.
Monica	You can't bear me taking you in my stride.
	Pause
Gerald	I think it's a devious form of aggression.
	Pause
Monica	But you can't bear me taking you in your stride either.
Gerald	I don't think I quite . . . follow that.
Monica	I don't know whether I do. *(Pause)* It sounded perspicacious when I said it. *(Pause)* Witty, even.
Gerald	I *always* find wit enigmatic.
Monica	Julie isn't witty. But she's—acute. Yes. Odd. Being both acute *and* muddleheaded.
Gerald	I think wit is a dangerous form of self-congratulation.
Monica	Perhaps Ben is very simple. Simple people do develop hysteria in relation to a certain *type.*
Gerald	Is Julie that type?
Monica	Is Ben hysterical?
Gerald	He throws things at her. Locks her out. Gets drunk and smashes the furniture. Always bursting into tears on those occasions.
Monica	And you think his motivations for all that are obscure?
Gerald	Well—
Monica	What if he's simply damned, bloody, annoyed with her most of the time? What I mean. What if she's simply damned, bloody, annoying most of the time?
Gerald	She's a rather placid person.
Monica	Could you imagine anything more damned bloody annoying than *that*?
Gerald	Aren't I placid? Do I annoy you?
Monica	People do different things with their annoyance. It would bore me to cry, and smash furniture. And if I threw things at you, I'd miss. Which wouldn't be satisfactory. *(Pause)* When I was sixteen, my gym mistress said: your physical co-ordination is not of the best, Monica. *(Pause)* I couldn't hit balls, and things like that. Couldn't get them through hoops, and those funny dangling sort of baskets. As for vaulting horses. . . .

Gerald	Bad at that too?
Monica	I used to wonder quite a lot how *boys* dared—
Gerald	Yes. It's not so bad for girls if they land on the crutch. *(Pause)* Yes. *(Pause)* I was frightened of vaulting horses, I'll admit.
Monica	I wasn't *frightened* of anything—
Gerald	More—inadequate.
Monica	No-o—
Gerald	Incompetent—
Monica	Definitely not.
Gerald	Can't think of any other words.
Monica	I can. I was disdainful.
Gerald	That makes sense. In the context.
Monica	Shall we get divorced?
Gerald	I think I've always been intimidated by your disdain.
Monica	For you?
Gerald	It in general. I can cope with it specifically. But not in general. It's a question of your behaviour versus your character.
Monica	If only we didn't discuss getting divorced so *often*! *(Pause)* The children don't give a damn. Judged by the way they conduct *their* lives, divorce is practically an act of saintly penitence.
Gerald	Did Clarry ring today?
Monica	Yes. The man aborted her, took his money, then got her a taxi. *(Pause)* Take it easy for a few days, he said.
	Pause
Gerald	And Tom?
Monica	He flounced out at seven, looking very Carnaby Street and sulky. *(Pause)* For someone who *isn't* queer, he gives a very dodgy impression that boy.
	Pause
Gerald	He probably is.
	Pause
Monica	Queer?
Gerald	Mmm.
Monica	He's capable of going that way out of sheer spite.
	Pause

Gerald	Do you think we despise Clarry and Tom?
Monica	Not at all. It's resentment. And *that's* because they've turned out badly and we feel guilty.
Gerald	Wouldn't say Clarry's turned out *badly.*
Monica	Messily. A bit like your Julie.
Gerald	What it is—Julie makes me feel nostalgic.
Monica	Jesus wept!
Gerald	She wouldn't go in for abortions, either.
Monica	Now if you're going to start getting at Clarry—
Gerald	I've nothing *against* abortions. Bloody hell. I paid for it didn't I?
Monica	Yes. And I thought you were curiously eager to do so. Something nasty *there,* Gerald.
Gerald	She wanted it didn't she? You accepted her point of view. *I* did. *(Pause)* You're beginning to make me feel as if I aborted her myself!
	Pause
Monica	I'm glad you see what I mean.
Gerald	If I paid Tom's gambling debts would that turn me into a roulette wheel?
Monica	I've *always* thought your devotion to Clarry a bit nasty. Still. I can see how you've tried to cope.
Gerald	How?
Monica	By bedding that succession of girls in your department.
Gerald	I do loathe that expression "bedding". If you're going to be crude—be cruder. What's more, I wish the idea of the unconscious mind had never been thought of. I'm not interested in any sort of casual relationship between my feelings for Clarry and my feelings for—other people. I don't deny the existence of things like that— it's simply that I don't feel illuminated by it. I also "bed" girls because I just like it. Enjoy it. Positively revel in it. *(Pause)* But haven't yet with Julie.
Monica	We really must get divorced.
	Pause
Gerald	One thing I will say for divorce, it's as cheap as an abortion.
Monica	You're so immature, Gerald!
Gerald	Do you know what maturity is?

Monica	What?
Gerald	It's behaviour determined by the plans other people have in mind for you.
Monica	Ho ho.
Gerald	Ho ho.

Pause

Monica	There's always the possibility that you're seriously interested in her. I think I'm still attractive, but it'd be a pretty good swap all the same for somebody of your age.

Pause

Gerald	Have *you* got your eye on anyone?
Monica	My eye tends to . . . flit about. But unlike you, I have the disadvantage of being fastidious.

Pause

Gerald	Monica—
Monica	What?
Gerald	How *many* years have we been talking to each other like this?
Monica	Years and years. Ever since you had your first chick, or dolly, or whatever they call them nowadays.
Gerald	I wonder what the masculine of chick and dolly is?
Monica	I don't hate you or anything. I don't even dislike you. I don't even not love you. It's just that you've become . . . microscopic to me. D'you see what I mean darling? Lots and lots of tiny details. I've got you *terrifically* in focus—

Pause

Gerald	Mmm.

Pause

Monica	Oddly enough, you still amaze me. Like things do, when you see them through a microscope. *(Pause)* I suppose amazement is as good a basis for marriage as any—

Pause

Gerald	I can't see you *at all.*
Monica	On the other hand, when one adds your details *up*—the effect is rather depressing. Sort of anonymous.
Gerald	I don't mean anything obvious, like familiarity. But I just can't see you.

Monica	What a pity. I'm still quite vivid, after my fashion. *I* think I'm *very visible.* It's you. You've acquired a blind spot. A bloody big one, too. *(Pause)* Do you think it could be something superficial? Like say your being very preoccupied with Julie?
Gerald	'Fraid not. No. Logically impossible.
Monica	*Logically?*
Gerald	What I mean—the condition antedates Julie. Anyway she doesn't preoccupy me. She obsesses me. I think. *(Pause)* Yes. *(Pause)* That's why I haven't actually done anything with her if you see what I mean. I'm so *obsessed*—that I can't come to terms with the actual person. *(Pause)* Poor old Julie.
Monica	Do you think she'd agree to be—what do they call it?— the Named Woman?
Gerald	Might. If we'd had—what do they call it?—sexual intercourse.
Monica	Well. That *is* something you can do. Isn't it. Up to a point.
Gerald	Don't be sly, Monica.
Monica	Of course, I could name her couldn't I, with or without her agreement? That's what I like about divorces. You can ignore people's *wills* with them.
Gerald	I will not have you imply that I'm losing my sexual piquancy! *(Pause)* It isn't that the implication makes me feel angry, or anxious, or threatened. No. It's simply a position I have adopted, that I won't have you imply it.
Monica	Unconscious fears of castration.
Gerald	No one could define their attitude to the unconscious more clearly than I have. I'm dug in there, and you can't undermine me. *(Pause)* I believe Jean-Paul Sartre is of the same opinion. *(Pause)* I am a kind of *machine.* Complicated—I'll give you that. But still a *mechanism.* If we hadn't had to invent the unconscious, we wouldn't have needed it.
Monica	Let me see. If we're going to get divorced, could you move out of the flat by Thursday? *(Gerald merely stares)* Could *she* ditch *Ben* by Thursday?
Gerald	She can't ditch him at all. He's too violent. *(Pause)* He might kill me. *(Pause)* I hear I'm down for a C.B.E., by the way.

Monica   You don't love her at all. It's that she puzzles you.
          You're a sucker for women who puzzle you. *(Pause)*
          The irony of it is—she isn't *puzzling. (Pause)* But I don't
          think I can take more than a few more days of you. I'm
          glad she's brought things to a head. *(Pause)* I'll tell you
          what. We'll make it a *week* on Thursday, and this
          weekend you can take her off somewhere and *try* her.
          If she doesn't work, I promise I won't throw you out
          lightly. All right?

Gerald   All right.

Monica   Not that I want you to be calculating about her. I don't
          want you to let either of you down, Gerald. That sort of
          thing can be very binding when people aren't married.

Gerald   I realise that.

                    Pause

Monica   Does she know how peculiar you are?

Gerald   I believe I do intrigue her a little.

Monica   But is it because of your *peculiarities?*

Gerald   Julie is profoundly attracted by things she doesn't
          understand. She identifies incomprehensibility with
          stature, one might say.

Monica   *(rising)* A week on Thursday then?

Gerald   Right.

                    Pause

Monica   Goodnight.

Gerald   Goodnight.

                    Monica exits

SCENE 3

          A hotel bedroom with an adjoining bathroom.
          The door opens—Gerald and Julie are ushered
          in by a porter carrying two small cases. He puts
          them down and goes out. Julie stands looking
          steadily at Gerald for a moment

Julie   I'm sorry about my face.

Gerald   I'm sorry *for* your face.

Julie   They say there won't be a scar.

Gerald   Hasn't Ben tried to get in touch with you somehow?

Julie   At the office. *(Crosses to bed and sits down)* He cries
           and says how sorry he is. Says he nearly killed himself
           that night. *(Pause)* He didn't know where I went or
           anything. Says he wants me to go back. *(Pause)* Where
           did you tell Monica you were going this weekend?

Gerald   With you.

Julie   Honestly?

Gerald   Honestly.

Julie   Thank God Ben doesn't know where *I* am. *(Pause)* Ben
           can do something like that . . . with the knife . . . then
           what he needs most of all is to be punished for it. Well.
           There he is alone, and I'm not there to punish him.
           (Pause) It'll be quite frustrating, don't you think? *(She
           smiles).*

Gerald   *Very* frustrating.

Julie   *(touches her wounded cheek)* He's more upset about
           this than I am. Does Monica think you and I've already
           been to bed together?

Gerald   She assumed it. I denied it. For once, I think, she didn't
           know what to believe. Monica's not so much interested
           in the truth, as in what she's decided to believe.

Julie   What happens when she decides wrong and finds out?

Gerald   She feels that whoever was involved has been obscurely
           cheating her.

Julie   That's what I'd feel.

                     Gerald looks at her and laughs. She laughs

Gerald   Are you hungry?

Julie   Yes. I'm sorry.

Gerald   Sorry why?

Julie   That was an enormous dinner we had. *(Pause)* I feel sort
           of sick and hungry at the same time.

Gerald   To do with being here with me?

Julie   Yes.

Gerald   Is it a good idea to eat then?

Julie   Yes. That's how I work.

Gerald   Coffee and sandwiches?

Julie   Yes, please.

                     Gerald takes his top coat off, picks up the
                     phone and orders coffee and sandwiches. Julie

> *stands up and slowly unbuttons her coat. She
> doesn't remove it*

Gerald   Aren't you going to take it off?

Julie   I've stayed in hotels with Ben. We always called
          ourselves Mr. and Mrs. Whittaker. You can't do it abroad
          though because of the passports.

Gerald   Which bit do you mean you can't do?

Julie   The Whittaker bit. Nobody ever tried to make us have
          separate rooms.
                    Pause

Gerald   Why Whittaker?

Julie   I don't know. Ben's idea. He said it sounds more like us
          than either of our own names. He thinks you should
          always lie about anything even remotely official.
          (Removes her coat) He's a kind of anarchist.

Gerald   He would be, wouldn't he?

Julie   I see what you mean.

Gerald   What are you?

Julie   Something like confused communist but no illusions. I
          think that covers it.

Gerald   Party member?

Julie   I'm not interested in the communist *party*. Anyway,
          joining things isn't my temperament. *(Pause)* It's too
          unequivocal. *(Pause)* I'm muddled, you see. I wish I was
          Vietnamese. I think I'd know where I stood then.

Gerald   I signed us in here under my own name.

Julie   On principle?

Gerald   I don't think I've *got* any principles.

Julie   People in the department think you have. You're
          regarded as having very *stern* ones. Incorruptible. They
          say it's your principles and your brilliant mind have got
          you to the top. *(Pause)* At the same time, they think
          you're a self-interested *bastard*. What do you make of
          that?
                    Pause

Gerald   I've got convictions.

Julie   It'll take us an extremely long time to get to know each
          other. Properly.

Gerald	And I've got twenty more years to communicate than you have.
Julie	But you've had some practice, haven't you?
Gerald	What do you mean?
Julie	Well. You've had quite a few young women, haven't you? So you must be quite experienced at getting yourself across.
Gerald	Oh.
Julie	Whereas, I've only had Ben and he's only three years older than me. I know two of the girls you've had, and —
Gerald	*(cuts in)* I do wish you wouldn't keep saying "had" and "have". It makes me feel squalid.
Julie	It's vernacular English.
Gerald	I'm talking about the *effect* on me.
Julie	I don't mind using a swear-word expression if you'd prefer that. I tend to sound priggish occasionally, but I'm not.

> *A waiter enters with the coffee and sandwiches. Puts them on a table. Exits. Gerald takes off his jacket. Julie takes a sandwich, bites at it and pours the coffee*

Julie	I like hotel sandwiches.
Gerald	Do you think we're quite ourselves this evening?
Julie	How d'you mean?
Gerald	I mean, do you think we're like what we've been like together before? *(Pause)* What a bloody ramshackle sentence!
Julie	We've never been in a private place before.
Gerald	So you do think we're a bit different!
Julie	Are you nervous?
Gerald	No.
Julie	I'm not either. I've noticed before. I can get to feel quite business-like about emotional things.
Gerald	Is that what you feel now? Businesslike?
Julie	My mouth's full of bread and ham. I'm not sure *what* I feel.
Gerald	Well swallow it down then.
Julie	That's what I'm trying to do. That's what eating *is,* isn't it?

Pause

Gerald	I'm beginning to feel tetchy.
Julie	Have a sandwich.
Gerald	No thanks.
Julie	I've poured you some coffee.

Gerald takes his coffee and goes to the window

| Gerald | I like the Suffolk coast. |
| Julie | What you're thinking is that I could be pretty maddening — aren't you? |

Pause

Gerald	The notion drifted across my mind. But it wasn't a discovery. I've realised it for some time. *(Pause)* Weeks ago.
Julie	So it hasn't put you off, then?
Gerald	Hardly, when I'm leaving Monica for you.
Julie	You make it sound sacrificial.
Gerald	You didn't leave Ben for me.
Julie	I would have. Ben and I lived in a chronic process of leaving each other. I suppose I needed something outside us to help me do it. Him as well. *(Pause)* I *would* have left him for you Gerald.
Gerald	I think you're picking up nuances of resentment that I'm not experiencing.

Pause

| Julie | Oh. |

Pause

Gerald	What's known as projection.
Julie	I know.
Gerald	The unconscious works in mysterious ways, etcetera. *(Pause)* Its wonders to perform.
Julie	Yes.
Gerald	I think I shall get ready for bed.
Julie	So will I.

Pause

| Gerald | Does your face hurt? |
| Julie | No, but I have to sleep on my back or the other side. And when I sleep on my back, I grind my teeth all night. *(Pause)* Ben says it's my aggressions coming out. *I think* |

it's something to do with the angle of my jaws when I'm
lying on my back. The bottom one's bound to hang,
isn't it? So my unconscious grinds them together to stop
them falling apart.

>   *Pause*

Gerald   Very logical.

Julie   If it wakes you up, what you have to do is punch me on
          the shoulder.

Gerald   Right.

>   *He opens his case, throws pyjamas on the bed,
>   and goes into the bathroom with his wash pack
>   leaving the door partly open*

Julie   I don't suppose you shave at night?

>   *Gerald puts his head round the bathroom door*

Gerald   Why?

Julie   I like to watch people shaving.

>   *Pause*

Gerald   Ben?

Julie   Yes. I used to sit and have a pee and watch him shave.

>   *Gerald comes into the room*

Gerald   I've often wished Monica needed to shave. That's
          something *I'd* like to watch.

>   *And he goes back into the bathroom. Turns on
>   the taps loudly. Julie wanders round the room,
>   examining everything very carefully. She goes
>   to the window and looks out. Sits on the bed—
>   slowly pushes off one shoe against the other,
>   then scrapes off the remaining shoe along the
>   floor. She plays with the shoes with her feet.
>   Gerald enters*

Gerald   Pyjamas—

Julie   Where?

Gerald   You're sitting on them.

>   *She tugs them from underneath her and hands
>   them over*

Julie   Nice pyjamas.

Gerald   *You* don't seem to be making much progress.

Julie   I've got my shoes off.

Gerald	Yes. *Very* sexy.
Julie	Do you know why I took to you in the first place?
Gerald	I've speculated in vain.
Julie	It was that article you published about socialism and town planning. Then I read your books. Then I tried to fit all that with what I'd seen and heard of you. Not that I'd *seen* much. The remote boss, and all that.
Gerald	*Did* it fit?
Julie	You were rotten to me at my promotion board.
Gerald	You do sort of *glare* in those situations Julie.
Julie	I glare because I'm frightened. I mean *when* I'm frightened.
Gerald	I wish I had the knack of being demonstrative.
Julie	Why?
Gerald	Because I sniff an incipient quarrel.
Julie	*I'm* not feeling quarrelsome—
Gerald	Neither am I.
Julie	Well then.
Gerald	But we *are* under a strain.
Julie	Are we? We must have put in scores of talking-hours. It isn't as if we didn't know each other at all. Or as if it was an impulse. Or just having a bit of sex. *(Pause)* Is it?
Gerald	Curious thing is—I don't feel very much like *myself*. I'm watching my behaviour for signs I can recognise, and I don't think I'm seeing any. Mind you I feel precarious about this at the best of times. *(Pause)* I have a suspicion that Monica and I have somehow evacuated each other's personalities.
Julie	Where to?
Gerald	*Eh?*
Julie	Well—*evacuated* you said. Where has it gone? What you were before you did it. If you see what I mean.
	Pause
Gerald	I don't know.
	Pause
Julie	I *always* feel like myself.
Gerald	That must be very reassuring.
Julie	Don't be mean.

Gerald   You know — I think I *am* mean. I've *grown* mean. I'm
          practically a work of art in that respect.

Julie   And Monica's the artist!

Gerald   Ho ho.

Julie   Ho ho.

Gerald   I wouldn't dream of saying she's responsible.

Julie   Would you dream of thinking it?

          Pause

Gerald   I told you there was a quarrel in the air!

          He makes for the bathroom door

Julie   Gerald — *(He turns)* Maybe we should have . . . er . . .
          slept together right from the start.

Gerald   I do detest that expression "sleeping together". It's
          worse than the other. It's nauseating.

Julie   *(tentatively)* Made love?

Gerald   Even worse.

          Pause

Julie   There's no expression sort of . . . neutral. Is there?

Gerald   I wish you'd get undressed!

Julie   D'you mean because you want to look at me.

Gerald   No. It's just that it would constitute — in my eyes, that is
          — a kind of progress.

Julie   There you are, you see! "In my eyes". There's your
          unconscious giving the show away.

Gerald   I haven't *got* a bloody unconscious!

          *And he stalks into the bathroom, closing the
          door. Julie stands up and takes her blouse off.
          She is wearing a slip underneath. Goes to the
          telephone and lifts the receiver*

          Pause

Julie   Would it be possible to send up a bottle of whisky. Yes.
          (Pause) Yes. A *bottle. (Pause)* Thank you very much.

          Gerald's head appears round the door

Gerald   Were you on the phone?

Julie   I've ordered some glug.

Gerald   What kind of glug.

Julie   Whisky.

Gerald   Anybody'd think you were a bloody virgin!

Julie	There's no connection in *me* between whisky and sexual anxiety. Maybe you're projecting.
Gerald	It was you ordered the booze.
	Pause
Julie	I take your point.
Gerald	*Good.*
	He withdraws. Julie goes to the bed, sits down and begins to take off her stockings. A waiter enters with the whisky — Julie pulls her skirt down. He eyes her impassively — and she him. In silence, he puts down the whisky and two glasses — takes away the coffee things. As the door closes behind him:
Julie	Good night.
	She awkwardly gets off one stocking and sits staring at her bare leg. Gerald enters in pyjamas. He goes to the other side of the bed and gets in:
Julie	I'm sorry you're uneasy.
Gerald	I didn't say so.
Julie	You got undressed *(pointing)* in *there*.
Gerald	I'm *not* uneasy.
Julie	*I* feel as if we've been married about ten years.
Gerald	Was it a successful marriage?
Julie	*(turns, smiling)* Very.
	Pause
Gerald	Such anxieties as I have centre round my paunch, really. It's not much — but enough to be a source of shame. Intellectually, I've destroyed the problem. But emotionally, it refused to wither away.
Julie	Why don't you wither the paunch away.
Gerald	Can't be bothered.
	Pause
Julie	Anyway, I like them.
Gerald	Why are you staring at your leg?
Julie	It suddenly seemed to me a most improbable object.
Gerald	They are. The arms as well. *(Pause)* The lot.
Julie	At least my legs aren't hairy. *(Pause)* Monica's are. *(Pause)* You could have got her to shave *them*.

Gerald	I did get her to shave them. Quite often. *(Pause)* And watched. *(Pause)* I believe she thought I was afflicted with some minor perversion about it.

Julie removes her other stocking

Julie	Do you think I'll get on with your children?
Gerald	Fortunately, my children regard "getting on" as something entirely superfluous to human relationships.
Julie	You do talk about them disparagingly.
Gerald	Yes. I know. It's a way of not acknowledging that I'm quite fond of them.
Julie	Why *not* acknowledge it?
Gerald	They've conditioned me over the years to regard my affection for them as a particularly noxious form of sentimentality. *(Pause)* One can't rebel against one's *children.*

Julie continues to sit, rather vacantly staring in front of her

Gerald	Would you mind passing me that book out of my case?
Julie	Your *book*?
Gerald	It's clear you're one of those people who can only get to bed in stages. I'm not criticising you. On the other hand, if I read it might make you feel uncomfortable. And when that sensation gets really acute, you might finish undressing and get into bed.

Julie gets his book and gives it to him

Julie	I don't like her novels.
Gerald	Neither do I. But if my criterion for what I read were my enjoyment, I'd be a moron.

Julie stands, and takes off her skirt

Julie	Have you ever had a girl on the carpet in your office?
Gerald	Several times. Not "had". Cohabited with.
Julie	"Cohabited's" worse than any of the others!
Gerald	I was being wry. Unfortunately, wryness is a brand of humour which depends utterly upon the other person's mental agility. Wryness has the disadvantage of not having punch lines.
Julie	Are you feeling more like you yet?

Pause

Gerald	I suddenly feel depressingly like me.

Julie takes her slip off. Underneath, she is
wearing a two-piece bathing costume.
Gerald sits up, staring in disbelief. Julie turns

Julie   What's the matter?

Gerald   Is that a bathing costume?

Julie   Yes.

Gerald   Are we going swimming?

Julie   I know it seems eccentric. But—

Pause

Gerald   But?

Pause

Julie   Well it *is* one of my eccentricities. *(Pause)* Every now and then, I put a swimming suit on instead of underwear.

Pause

Gerald   *Why?*

Julie   If I had a reason, it wouldn't be eccentric. Would it?

Gerald   I think there's a tenable case either way.

Pause

Julie   That was why I was so slow getting undressed. You see. Because I had *this* on underneath. *(Pause)* And I didn't know what you'd make of it.

Pause

Gerald   Why didn't *you* go in the bathroom.

Julie   I decided that would be dishonest.

Gerald   Isn't it rather uncomfortable? I mean, with clothes?

Julie   Yes.

Pause

Gerald   How did . . . how did *Ben* used to react?

Julie   Quaintly, is the word I'd use to describe his reaction. He said it was an inverted form of whorishness in me. Then he'd get really worked up about whorishness in women in general. Then he'd lose his temper. And *then* he'd throw something at me.

Pause

Gerald   I see.

Pause

Julie   There's quite a lot of things about me that I don't understand, and irritate other people. I know what they

all are. I'm as bewildered and irritated as any of you.
(Pause) But *I'm* quite adjusted to them. They're what
help me to feel like me all the time, like I said. *(Pause)*
I'm very stubborn about them.

>   *Pause*

Gerald   I think it's charming.

>   *Julie begins putting on her slip*

Gerald   What are you doing?

Julie   Getting dressed.

Gerald   You mean, you're going to come to bed *dressed.*

Julie   I'm not *that* eccentric.

Gerald   And when you've got dressed?

Julie   I don't know yet. I had one of my mental flashes.

Gerald   Mental flashes —

Julie   Insights. *(Pause)* It's all to do with the unconscious.

Gerald   So I've heard.

>   *She puts her blouse on, then her skirt. Gerald*
>   *watches fascinatedly*

Julie   I try never to act inconsistently with my insights. I trust
                them. *(Pause)* Other people often find it very
                inconvenient of me.

Gerald   Well I expect it very often *is* inconvenient. *(Pause)* Like
                now.

Julie   It's no good my apologising, because I don't feel
                apologetic.

Gerald   Yes. I think I can follow that.

>   *Julie completes her dressing. She touches her*
>   *cheek*

Julie   My cut started to hurt.

Gerald   And it reminded you of dear old Ben, and the happy
                days together.

Julie   That's cheap, Gerald.

Gerald   Extremely. It's because I'm very angry. And whenever I
                have a genuine emotion, I tend to disfigure it with
                cheapness. *(Pause)* That's partly what I meant about
                being mean. *(Pause)* I'm mean spirited. *(Pause)* Is that
                what was in your mental flash?

>   *Pause*

Julie   Yes.

Gerald   I thought so. All that's left of me is posthumous
            remains of what once might have been a genuine
            identity. *(Pause)* A complementary process has taken
            place in my wife.

Julie   Are you being self-pitying?

Gerald   Not at all. Monica and I are quite fascinating, and
            complex — in our withered fashion. *(Pause)* You can't
            play *my* games. *(Pause)* I wondered if you'd catch on.

Julie   Are you hurt?

Gerald   Of course I'm hurt. I love you and I want to live with
            you.

                       Pause

Julie   I love you, too.

Gerald   Then what do you suggest? For the time being?

Julie   What do *you* suggest?

                       Gerald swings his legs out of bed, onto the floor.
                       Looks at his watch

Gerald   *I* rather fancy a midnight drive. *(Pause)* Back to London.

                       SCENE 4

                       Gerald and Monica's flat. They sit at breakfast.
                       A bright, sunny morning

Monica   You do look grey, Gerald.

Gerald   No sleep. Couldn't, in the armchair. And didn't want
            to wake you.

Monica   A sort of muddy colour. And you need a shave. Little
            black prickles all over. *(Pause)* There are flecks of
            mucous in the corners of your mouth.

Gerald   I'm sure there are.

Monica   Drink your orange juice, then —

                       He does so. Monica is sipping black coffee

Gerald   You look very well.

                       Pause

Monica   I had a good night. I was half expecting you back, as a
            matter of fact.

Gerald   Did you have an insight about it?

Monica   I think it might have been an insight. *(Pause)* Something
            to do with being quite well aware that you've always

been faithful to me. *(Pause)* I've never *seriously* thought otherwise, you know.

Gerald I know.

> *Pause*

Monica My anxieties haven't been about whether—but why not.

Gerald I see.

Monica Clarry's last man but one had me *(Pointing)* over there. On the couch. *(Pause)* When we'd finished, he said: by the way, have you had the menopause?

Gerald Cheek.

Monica I've been unfaithful on and off, for years. *(Pause)* How things went round and round in my little head! Wondering if you sort of *knew*, you see. And wondering whether you were doing the same and were wondering whether *I* knew. *(Pause)* But I knew you weren't.

> *Pause*

Gerald How?

Monica I know you too well, Gerald.

Gerald Ah!

Monica I'll admit *this* time you had me worried. By actually going off, I mean.

Gerald Still. You knew it would turn out all right.

Monica I *think* so.

> *Pause*

Gerald Why didn't you have one of yours in last night?

Monica I thought about it. Then I realised that knowing you were with Julie, I wanted to feel above it for a day or two.

Gerald To feel chaste, as it were.

Monica As it were.

> *Pause*

Gerald About *your* infidelities—

Monica Quaint word—

Gerald You are lying.

Monica I'm not, darling. *(Pause)* I used our infighting about *yours* as a kind of cover. Didn't I encourage you, after all, to bring that series of girls here from the Ministry? Those poor little girls you said lived in bed-sitters and didn't eat well enough. *(Pause)* For roast leg of lamb, strawberries and Bartok. *(Pause)* Talking of Bartok — when you were in Hungary, I had a Hungarian. Isn't that a coincidence?

Gerald	*Had?*
Monica	Sorry. Copulated with.

    Pause

Gerald	I was quite sincere about those girls.
Monica	Consciously!

    Pause

Gerald	*I* might have had a Hungarian when I was in Hungary —
Monica	But you didn't.
Gerald	I nearly did.
Monica	There you are. That's what I *mean* about you Gerald.
Gerald	What is?
Monica	There aren't any rules in sex. You're a bad case of *rules.*
Gerald	I have no moral positions vis-a-vis sex *whatsoever.*
Monica	Not in theory, I'll grant you. But in practice —
Gerald	Don't you want to know why Julie and I came back?
Monica	Would it be interesting?

    Pause

Gerald	Her part of it is complicated, I think. Mine is very simple.
Monica	A lack of lust —

    Pause

Gerald	*Eh?*
Monica	You lack *lust*, Gerald.
Gerald	I think I can say that's something I have more than anybody's fair share of.
Monica	Then where do you keep it all the time?

    Pause

Gerald	Inside.
Monica	Why?
Gerald	I've no option. It doesn't seem to be able to get out. *(Pause)* But it's *there.*
Monica	Where?

    Pause

Gerald	It's very hard to convey to someone the *topography* of an emotion.
	Pause
Monica	But it nearly popped out when you were in Hungary.
Gerald	Very nearly.
Monica	What was she like?
	Pause
Gerald	Huge. *(Pause)* Attractive though.
Monica	You see. Those girls you brought here — I'm afraid you *didn't* lust after them.
Gerald	How do you know?
Monica	I can tell.
Gerald	How can you know what goes on with me *inside*?
Monica	Because I know you inside out.
Gerald	They did live in bed-sitters. They didn't eat properly. They were charming — each and every one of them. *(Pause)* Sensitive. Educated. Good looking.
Monica	They hated Bartok. Each and every one of them.
Gerald	*I* hate Bartok.
Monica	No. I'm sorry. They were a wretched lot, Gerald. Neurotic . . . frigid —
Gerald	*Frigid*?
Monica	You have an unconscious preference for frigid women. It works both ways. *They* don't threaten your fears of impotence, and *you* don't threaten their fears of defloration.
	Pause
Gerald	Were they virgins then?
Monica	How should I know?
Gerald	Well I mean. They'd need to be, wouldn't they? In order to have fears about def —
Monica	I assure you an experienced woman can have those fears. You will be so *literal* Gerald!
Gerald	Yes. All it is — it's just me picking at the *logic* of the thing.
Monica	Anyway. Hah!
	Pause
Gerald	Try to be explicit. For God's sake, *try*!

Monica	You soon came scuttling back from Suffolk last night!
Gerald	Look at your face!
Monica	What?
Gerald	I've just seen it.
Monica	*What*?
Gerald	It looks to me like a face that's been gloating for a very long time — then suddenly given up for sinister reasons it won't let on.
Monica	I've never done any of my gloating on my *face*!
	Pause
Gerald	*Where*, then?
Monica	Nor inside neither.
	Pause
Gerald	The curious thing is — I don't feel betrayed because of your betrayals. I feel betrayed because of not knowing.
Monica	Nonsense. People always know. Somewhere.
Gerald	There you go again! *Where*?
Monica	What about inside, love?
Gerald	How can I not know something I'm supposed to know inside? It doesn't make sense.
	Pause
Monica	If only, like the rest of the world, you'd take into account one's unconscious!
Gerald	Not the rest of the world. Half the world's communist. And *they* wouldn't have the unconscious if you threw it at them. No. And what's more —
Monica	Gerald —
Gerald	What?
Monica	You look quite demented.
Gerald	Lack of sleep.
Monica	That girl must be a fool.
Gerald	She's certainly very odd.
Monica	I loathe teasers!
Gerald	She didn't tease me. She just changed her mind, for reasons which I could follow without any trouble.
	Pause
Monica	Well? Go on.
Gerald	There was something about me that disturbed her.

Monica   That sounds plausible enough!

Gerald   It transcends plausibility. It's a fact.

Monica   I hope you escaped without humiliation? Don't you
          want any of your ginger marmalade?

Gerald   I'm not having ginger marmalade this morning.

Monica   Anyone who knows you *at all* can see there's something
          disturbing about you. You're a bewildered, desiccated
          wreck with pathetic sexual fantasies that paralyse you
          out of your wits.
                    Pause

Gerald   I think — taking things by and large, as they say — I am of
          that opinion myself.

Monica   I'm sure you are. No one's accusing you of any lack of
          self-awareness.
                    *She gets up and begins to gather things
                    together on the table ready to clear it. On the
                    corner by Gerald's elbow there is a breadboard
                    with bread and a long, slender carving knife
                    which they use as a breadknife.*
                    Gerald's glance rests on it for a moment.

Gerald   The question is —
                    Pause

Monica   What's the question?
                    Pause

Gerald   Am I entirely a self-made product in those respects you
          mentioned?

Monica   What do you think?
                    Pause

Gerald   I'm sadly of another opinion. Which is that I can't
          evade responsibility for what I am. There may be an
          objective case for such an evasion, but I'm hardly in a
          position to make it. Am I?

Monica   *(comes close to him)* For a minute, I thought you were
          going to say what you are is *my* fault!

Gerald   Nothing of the kind.

Monica   Well. At least you're not a hypocrite. *(Looks at his plate)*
          Have you finished?

Gerald   Yes.

> *She leans across him to take his plate. As she
> does so, Gerald takes the breadknife and
> neatly thrusts it into her. She collapses across
> him. He picks her up and takes her to the
> couch—puts her down. She is dead. He goes to
> the telephone and dials*

Gerald   I want the police, if I may—

SCENE 5

> *Fade in Julie and Ben's room. Evening. Julie
> sits by the fire, huddled in her outdoor coat.
> Ben enters, carrying his violin case. He shuts
> the door behind him and leans against it. After
> a moment, when she does not turn to face him,
> he puts the case down and goes to her*

Ben   Julie—
> *Pause*

Julie   Yes. I'm back. You can start throwing things. *(Turning)*
           Knife's in the kitchen drawer.

> *He puts his hand out and touches her face where
> the cut is. She sits frozen*

Julie   Been for your violin lesson?

Ben   Yes.
> *Pause*

Julie   I've been on a dirty weekend.

> *Ben jerks his hand away. Steps back*

Ben   With Gerald?

Julie   Yes.
> *Pause*

Ben   So you thought you'd just pop in and let me know!

Julie   If you'll not lose your temper for a minute—

Ben   What do you *expect* me to do? Ask you if you enjoyed
           yourself?
> *Pause*

Julie   I didn't sleep with him—

Ben   What did you do? Play Bartok records?

Julie   I was going to. I mean sleep with him.

Ben	It's quite usual to do that, when you go away with somebody.
Julie	It was horrible.
Ben	*Intending* to was?
Julie	Being with him.
	Pause
Ben	Are you visiting, or what?
Julie	I'd like to come back. *(Pause)* You said on the phone you wanted me to come back.
Ben	And you said it was no use.
Julie	*(pointing at her cheek)* They had to put *stitches* in that!
Ben	Not many, by the look of it.
Julie	We went to Suffolk. On the coast. To a hotel. *(Pause)* He's a very intelligent man. *(Pause)* Well. We had dinner on the way. It's a funny thing, when he'd had a few glasses of wine his breath smelt like metal. Sort of gusts of metal smell blowing across the table when he talked. And when he eats, his cheeks cave in. Don't you think with food in them they'd sort of be full, at least. But they cave in.
Ben	Swallows without chewing!
Julie	He has dandruff, as well. I saw these little flakes drifting down into his soup. *He* saw them. He gave me quite a defiant stare. *(Pause)* I didn't refer to them.
Ben	Really flakes? Or just little bits?
Julie	Flakes.
Ben	Then he'll have eczema of the ears as well. Inside, you know. It can result in a chronic discharge.
Julie	I thought his ears looked his healthiest bit.
Ben	Do you expect me to calmly stand here talking about it?
Julie	No.
	Ben takes his coat off
Ben	I've been managirg very well on me own.
Julie	I'll try to be more submissive.
Ben	Look. I never *wanted* to brutalise you! There's just something about you that asks for it.
Julie	And there's something about you that wants me to ask for it!

She gets up and goes to look in the cupboard
where she kept her clothes. It is empty

Julie   Where's the rest of my clothes?

Ben   Burnt them.

Julie   *(closing cupboard)* I suppose that was to be expected.

Ben   Listen. When *I* start up with another woman, you can
        bloody burn mine. You won't get *me* complaining.
        If there's one thing I do understand, it's human
        aggressiveness. What's more —

Julie   I don't think I'd mind if you had somebody else.

Ben   Oh? How would *you* react?

Julie   I'd ignore it.

Ben   You don't seriously think I can believe that!

Julie   I'd ignore it.

Ben   You'd *seethe*, mate! I know you. You're one of those
        people that's adjusted to a personality they haven't got.
        I suppose when you went off with Gerald you really
        believed you were going to sleep with him?

Julie   *You* thought I was doing it *anyway*!

Ben   I'm talking about your lack of realism about your
        chronic behaviour patterns.

Julie   I may be unrealistic about them but I do try to
        overcome them. Which is more than you do.

Ben   Fists came before thoughts.

Julie   And how long did it take to evolve *knives*?

Ben   I don't *want* you back.

Julie   Hah! After all that histrionics on the telephone!

Ben   Next time I might kill you.

Julie   Well that's my risk isn't it?

Ben   It'd be me would do the life sentence.
                        Pause

Julie   I liked him. But he made me feel suicidal. *(Pause)* He
        undressed in the bathroom.

Ben   So you did get as far as undressing!

Julie   He did.

Ben   Not you, of course. You went down in full battle kit, I
        suppose?

Julie	You've already implied that I *couldn't* have believed I was going to sleep with him. Looked at in purely rational terms, I can't make your position out at all. Was I or wasn't I going to?
Ben	If *you* look at anything about me in rational terms, it just makes me want to punch you.
	Pause
Julie	I'm sorry for his wife.
Ben	Why?
Julie	She must feel so *guilty*.
Ben	Why?
Julie	When she sees what their marriage has turned him into.
Ben	*What* has it turned him into?
Julie	It's deformed him.
Ben	Physically, I hope.
Julie	Now listen—
Ben	And the usual thing? He turned to you because she doesn't understand him?
	Pause
Julie	He turned to me . . . because he understands himself.
Ben	What did he look like undressed? Sickening?
Julie	I only saw him with his pyjamas on.
Ben	With his pyjamas on then—
	Pause
Julie	Like a sort of—striped hen. *(Pause)* A *donnish* striped hen. And when I started getting undressed—
Ben	How far did you get?
Julie	Blouse, skirt, slip, stockings.
Ben	So you were in your bloody underwear then!
	Pause
Julie	I had my swimming costume on.
Ben	Was the man visibly shaken? Did he scream? Try to get away?
Julie	I'm trying to be serious, Ben—
Ben	Despite the facetious tone, I'm bloody serious.
Julie	The thing is, I got dressed again almost straight away. *(Pause)* And we came back to London.
	Pause

Ben	So. You stood in front of him half naked then!
Julie	If I'd been on a beach or somewhere —
Ben	You *weren't* on a beach, were you?
Julie	Don't be so petty!
Ben	Is that petty?
Julie	Well isn't it?
Ben	*Objectively* it's petty. *Subjectively* I've got some very nasty feelings coagulating round it.
Julie	Ben we didn't *do* anything —
Ben	I'm obsessed with the intention —
Julie	I could see afterwards I hadn't intended.
Ben	But you couldn't see it at the time?
Julie	No.
Ben	Then as far as I'm concerned you were intending. Now get out —
Julie	Please, Ben —

> *He rushes into the kitchen, grabs three cups and stands in the doorway with them*

Ben	Are you getting out?
Julie	Do you want me to?
Ben	If you provoke me any more I shall feel ludicrous. And you know what happens then!
Julie	If you hadn't cut me, I'd never have gone —
Ben	*Right*!

> *One after the other he hurls the three cups at her — they all miss, and break on the wall. They stand facing each other in silence for a long time, immobile*

Ben	*(quietly)* I *am* ludicrous. *(Pause)* Aren't I? *(Pause)* Why is that? I can *see* I'm ludicrous. *(Pause)* Why should genuine feelings come out ludicrous?

> *There is another long silence*

Julie	*(turning to the piano)* We never got started on that violin piano sonata —

> *Pause*

Ben	I promised myself — that if you came back, I'd control myself.

> *Julie sits down and tries a few bars of the*
> *Vivaldi violin piano sonata on the piano*
> *Pause*

Ben   Gerald gone back to his wife?

Julie   Yes. *(Pause)* Come on. Shall we try it?

Ben   The Vivaldi?

Julie   Yes.

> *Pause*

Ben   All right.

> *He gets out his violin, sets up his music stand*
> *and sits down ready to play. Tunes the violin*

Ben   Give me A then —

> *She gives him the note*

Ben   Right. Come on then. Let's murder Vivaldi.

> *They continue to play*

End